TECHNICAL REPORT

A Survey of Recent Qatari Secondary School Graduates

Methods and Results

Francisco Martorell • *Vazha Nadareishvili*

With
Hanine Salem

Prepared for the Supreme Education Council

RAND-QATAR POLICY INSTITUTE

The research described in this report was prepared for the Supreme Education Council and conducted within the RAND-Qatar Policy Institute and RAND Education, programs of the RAND Corporation.

Library of Congress Cataloging-in-Publication Data

Martorell, Francisco, 1963-
    A survey of recent Qatari secondary school graduates : methods and results / Francisco Martorell,
Vazha Nadareishvili. With Hanine Salem.
        p. cm.
    Includes bibliographical references.
    ISBN 978-0-8330-4472-3 (pbk. : alk. paper)
    1. Education, Secondary—Qatar. 2. High school graduates—Employment—Qatar. 3. Educational survey—
Qatar. I. Nadareishvili, Vazha. II. Salem, Hanine. III. Title.

LA1435.M37 2008
373.12'912095363—dc22

2008019238

Published 2008 by the RAND Corporation
1776 Main Street, P.O. Box 2138, Santa Monica, CA 90407-2138
1200 South Hayes Street, Arlington, VA 22202-5050
4570 Fifth Avenue, Suite 600, Pittsburgh, PA 15213-2665
RAND URL: http://www.rand.org/
To order RAND documents or to obtain additional information, contact
Distribution Services: Telephone: (310) 451-7002;
Fax: (310) 451-6915; Email: order@rand.org

Preface

The government of Qatar is embarking on a number of reforms to support the nation's economic and social development. Qatar's future depends on citizens whose education and training prepare them to be full participants in economic, social, and political life, and Qatar has made significant efforts to improve educational opportunities. Many efforts have focused on post-secondary education, but these individual initiatives have not been subject to a broader strategic review. Qatar's Supreme Education Council asked the RAND-Qatar Policy Institute (RQPI) to study the current situation and to help it identify priorities for developing post-secondary educational offerings that better respond to the country's economic and social demands.

This report presents the results of a survey of Qataris who left secondary school in 1998, to learn about their education and employment experiences since graduation. It was written as part of a larger, one-year study on post-secondary education in Qatar. The report should be of interest to those concerned with education and economic development issues in the Middle East. It should also serve as a resource for researchers interested in tabulations from the survey.

The main report from this project is *Post-Secondary Education in Qatar: Employer Demand, Student Choice, and Options for Policy,* by Cathleen Stasz, Eric Eide, and Francisco Martorell, MG-644-QATAR, 2007.

This project was conducted under the auspices of RQPI and RAND's Education unit. RQPI is a partnership of the RAND Corporation and the Qatar Foundation for Education, Science, and Community Development. The aim of RQPI is to offer the RAND style of rigorous and objective analysis to clients in the greater Middle East. In serving clients in the Middle East, RQPI draws on the full professional resources of the RAND Corporation. RAND Education analyzes education policy and practice and supports implementation of improvements at all levels of the education system.

For further information on RQPI, contact the director, Dr. Richard Darilek. He can be reached by email at redar@rand.org; by telephone at +974-492-7400; or by mail at P.O. Box 23644, Doha, Qatar. For more information about RAND Education, contact the associate director, Dr. Charles Goldman. He can be reached by e-mail at charlesg@rand.org; by telephone at +1-310-393-0411, extension 6748; or by mail at RAND, 1776 Main Street, Santa Monica, California 90401 USA.

Contents

Tables

Summary

The state of Qatar is a nation in transition. It is immensely wealthy because of its reserves of oil and natural gas, yet its leaders believe the country needs to develop a diversified, competitive economy (Nafi, 1983; Rathmell and Schulze, 2000). Through large investments in educational opportunities for its citizens, Qatar's leadership has made it clear that it sees a well-educated populace as key to achieving that goal. Despite this recognition, the nation faces a number of challenges as it moves into the 21st century. The system of widespread public-sector employment has resulted in a workforce that is overwhelmingly employed by the government and an economy highly dependent on foreign workers. And, although a wide array of educational offerings is available in Qatar, many employers and policymakers are concerned about the skills of students produced by the Qatari educational system.

Recognizing these problems, the Qatari leadership asked RAND to assess the current situation and help develop priorities for providing post-secondary educational offerings. One of the primary impediments policymakers face in devising effective ways to improve educational quality is lack of data. Census and labor force surveys contain useful information, but they have important limitations. First, they are conducted infrequently and irregularly. Qatar's first and second censuses were conducted in 1986 and 1997, and the latest census was conducted in 2004 (the most recent population-wide labor force survey was conducted in 2001). Perhaps more important, such surveys contain little or no information about the aspirations, experiences, and educational needs of young Qataris. This is precisely the information needed to shape effective educational reforms that serve individuals who are transitioning between school and their post-schooling lives. For example, policymakers deciding whether to expand educational offerings would benefit from knowing what the interests of young Qataris are as well as the areas where they might benefit from additional schooling.

To shed light on these issues, the RAND team conducted two surveys: one of current high school seniors and a second of young Qataris who graduated in 1998.[1] The main purpose of this report is to describe the survey of the 1998 high school graduates and to report summary tabulations, expanding on the data presented in the main report (Stasz, Eide, and Martorell, 2007).

---

[1] In addition to the surveys, we conducted interviews with employers and policymakers and reviewed 2004 census data and Planning Council data (See Planning Council, 2005).

Survey Design and Sampling Strategy

The target population for this survey was of Qataris who graduated from high school in 1998. We designed the survey to collect information on the transitions that members of this cohort made in the years between the end of high school and spring 2006. Specifically, the survey contained questions on family structure (e.g., marital status and number of children), post-secondary schooling, work and employment experiences, and attitudes about careers, school, and work.

Our goal was to obtain a final sample size of 100 respondents, with an equal share of men and women. Ultimately, we were able to survey 50 men and 49 women, for a total sample size of 99 respondents. To identify potential respondents, we used the Qatar Ministry of Education's (MoE's) administrative files, which contain information on which students graduated in each year. We randomly sampled individuals from that registry to generate the sample of graduates to be interviewed. The primary challenge we faced was contacting potential respondents. Our strategy was to use the phone number of the family home listed on the MoE data file. A serious limitation of this approach is that individuals who could be reached might differ systematically from those who could not. To assess the severity of this limitation, we compared the sample respondents to individuals in the underlying population from which they were drawn. We found that, in terms of high school field of study and eventual educational attainment, sample members did not differ substantially from individuals in the cohort as a whole. This finding suggests that our sample is reasonably representative of the underlying population.

What Are the Educational Experiences of Young Qataris?

More than 80 percent of the respondents continued studying after graduation from high school and more than 66 percent reported their current level of education was higher than a secondary degree. We found sharp differences between the educational attainment of men and women. Female respondents outperformed males in both pursuit of, and achievement in, post-secondary education. Only half of the men reported that their current level of schooling was beyond secondary school, compared with 80 percent of female respondents. Among respondents who had attended a post-secondary program, women were considerably more likely to have completed their degree program than men (85 percent compared with 58 percent). Overall, 71 percent of female respondents reported completing a university degree, compared with just 36 percent of male respondents.

We found other gender differences in post-secondary education as well. Some major fields of study (such as "Law" and "Engineering") were chosen only by men, while others ("Education" and "Humanities, arts, and literature") were pursued exclusively by women. Almost one-third of male survey participants went abroad for post-secondary education; all the females received post-secondary education in Qatar.

What Are the Main Employment Experiences of Young Qataris?

About two-thirds of the sample respondents were employed at the time of the survey. Not surprisingly, the employment rate exhibited a large gender gap, with nearly all men (88 percent) indicating they were employed, compared with only 54 percent of women. In fact, a sizable share of female respondents (43 percent) reported never having held a job since leaving high school, which shows that even among relatively young Qataris, many women either decide not to work or do not have the opportunity to do so.

The survey also asked a series of questions about the characteristics of the respondents' job. Virtually all employed sample members worked in a government ministry or for an establishment owned by the government (e.g., Qatar Petroleum), which is consistent with other research showing that Qataris overwhelmingly choose not to work in private-sector jobs (Planning Council, 2005). Respondents indicated that interpersonal skills (such as working in a group and giving/taking orders) and communication skills were important in their jobs. Notably, fluency in a foreign language was a widely cited skill, especially among men.

We also found that participation in formal job training (defined as training that does not occur at school or at a structured program at one's employment) to acquire these skills is common.[2] Nearly 60 percent of respondents indicated they received formal training to learn skills needed for their job. Training was even more widespread among respondents employed at a government corporation (75 percent).

Attitudes Toward Work and School

The responses to the attitudinal questions on work and school yielded some surprising results. Both male and female respondents felt that being made to feel respected and appreciated was the most important feature of a job.[3] In contrast, factors associated with financial compensation (salary and other monetary benefits) were ranked in the middle of the job characteristics that we considered. Another interesting finding was the relatively progressive attitudes about gender roles. A large majority (88 percent) of respondents agreed with the statement that there should be more jobs open to women. Even among men, this sentiment appears to be widely held (75 percent of male respondents agreed with the statement).

Implications

Methodologically, this report demonstrates the feasibility of conducting this type of survey in a similar setting.[4] The approach we used to identify sample respondents and to contact them worked reasonably well, even though the contact information that was available to us was about eight years out of date. This method was successful at least in part because Qatar is a relatively small, developed country where familial ties are strong. In settings where individuals are not easily reachable by mobile phone or where family ties are weaker, contact information that is very out of date may not be enough to locate potential respondents.

---

[2] An example would be foreign language training that occurs at a center devoted exclusively for this skill.

[3] The survey questions did not distinguish between respect from employers or co-workers and respect from family members or the rest of society.

[4] Stasz, Eide, and Martorell (2007) discuss at length the policy implications of many of the survey tabulations presented here. Because this report instead focuses on describing the survey methodology and presenting tabulations from the survey, it only briefly describes their policy implications.

The inherent drawbacks of this strategy underscore the need for obtaining information that can be used to assess whether the sample of respondents accurately reflects the sampled population. Although the results discussed in this report suggest that our sample is fairly representative of the underlying population, a limitation of our data is that we have relatively few characteristics that can be used to judge sample representativeness. Thus, we recommend that studies that conduct surveys using a similar strategy make acquiring such information a data collection priority.

The report also shows how this type of survey can be used to obtain information that is not available from other sources and that is useful for policymakers. For instance, we found that most respondents saw English language proficiency as a skill important to their job. This finding indicates that providing high-quality language instruction in schools and in job training centers is warranted. Another interesting result is that when indicating which job characteristics respondents saw as important, the respect conferred by a job outranked monetary compensation. This knowledge is helpful for policymakers interested in developing policies that foster greater willingness on the part of young Qataris to work in the private sector (Stasz, Eide, and Martorell, 2007).

Acknowledgments

This project would not have been possible without the cooperation of many individuals and organizations. First, we thank the Supreme Education Council (SEC), which gave full support to the project and helped us gain access to the MoE records we used to locate survey respondents.

A large international team carried out the survey, and the team's collective work contributed to this report. In Doha, the telephone interviews were carried out in a very short time frame by Eiman Al Ansari, Hessa Al Thani, Abdulrazaq Al Kuwari, Mie Al Missned, Louay Constant, and Hanine Salem (who also organized all the fieldwork). Joy Moini and Lawrence Tingson helped with post-interview data collection and processing. Hanine Salem and Eric Eide worked on the survey design and interview protocol, and Cathy Stasz provided a number of helpful suggestions that improved the data analysis. Charles Goldman, associate director of RAND Education, provided thoughtful input throughout the study. Cathy Stasz and Catherine Augustine gave us helpful suggestions for improving the text. Sharon Koga carried out various administrative duties.

Finally, we thank the individuals who participated in the anonymous telephone interviews and surveys.

Abbreviations

CIA	U.S. Central Intelligence Agency
ILO	International Labour Organization
ISCO	International Standard Classification of Occupations
MoE	Qatar Ministry of Education
RQPI	RAND-Qatar Policy Institute
SEC	Qatar Supreme Education Council

CHAPTER ONE

Introduction

The state of Qatar is a small nation with vast natural resource wealth. Although Qatar's economy is heavily dependent on sales of oil and natural gas (CIA, 2005), the nation's leadership is interested in diversifying the economy.[1] The government is also interested in expanding professional opportunities for women so that they can contribute to the nation's economic future (Brewer, Augustine, Zellman, et al., 2007).

Since education is a key component of a productive workforce, educational investments have been a top governmental priority. This is evidenced by the establishment of branch campuses of world class universities in Education City (Stasz, Eide, and Martorell, 2007). Despite these measures and sweeping reforms of the K–12 educational system (Brewer, Augustine, Zellman, et al., 2007), the general perception is that Qatar's K–12 and post-secondary systems do not produce graduates who have the tools to succeed in the global marketplace. In part because of these perceptions, Qatari employers generally prefer to hire expatriate workers, particularly for jobs requiring specialized education or training (Stasz, Eide, and Martorell, 2007).

Another challenge is the widespread availability of government employment (or employment in government-owned corporations (Planning Council, 2005). Such employment effectively serves as a mechanism to share the nation's natural resource wealth, which is an important social goal. However, it has a number of potentially perverse effects that impede progress toward a diversified, competitive economy, and it could reduce Qatari students' incentive to work hard in school, because the implicit employment guarantee is not contingent on holding an advanced degree or a specialized skill. Indeed, the poor academic performance of young men is a central concern of Qatari policymakers (Stasz, Eide, and Martorell, 2007).

Recognizing these problems, the Qatari leadership has sought to understand the steps it can take to help produce a better educated workforce that is positioned to enter, and succeed in, employment outside the public sector. Unfortunately, there is a shortage of data on which to base policy changes. In particular, apart from anecdotal evidence, little is known about the aspirations and experiences of young Qataris, even though this type of information is crucial for shaping reforms that effectively target the problems facing individuals who are just now entering the labor force. To examine these issues, we conducted two surveys, one of current high school seniors and a second of young Qataris who graduated in 1998. We also conducted interviews with employers and policymakers and reviewed existing census and labor market data.

---

[1] Qatar's reserves of natural resources are forecasted to last for over 100 years (Romero, 2005), making the impetus to diversify the economy much less strong than it is in other Gulf States (e.g., the United Arab Emirates).

The main findings from these analyses are discussed in Stasz, Eide, and Martorell (2007). This report serves as a description of the data collected from members of the 1998 high school graduation cohort (henceforth the "1998 cohort"). This survey was designed to gather information about the employment and educational plans and experiences of young Qatari adults. The data we collected are a resource that can be used to study a range of questions pertaining to this population. This data collection effort is unique in several ways:

- Although there are data collections with information on labor-market and educational experiences (e.g., census and national labor-market surveys), they do not specifically target young Qataris, and publicly available tabulations do not report results specific to this group.[2]
- Current data collections focus on objective experiences and circumstances (such as level of schooling) and do not have information on attitudes toward school and work.
- Our survey collected more-detailed information on labor market outcomes and educational experiences. For example, it asked about the skills required at the respondents' current job, as well as about whether the respondent studied abroad or in Qatar.
- We used high school administrative records to generate the sampling frame. Options such as census records were not available; other options, such as random digit dialing, would not be practical given the narrow sample criteria (recent high school graduates).
- Reaching sampled individuals was not straightforward because we did not have contact information for them. We used the parents' phone number from the high school records and then tried to reach the sampled individuals by calling their mobile phone if their parents provided it to us.

This report aims to provide the reader with an overview of the education and work experiences of young Qataris. Our intention is to offer a set of descriptive facts and to highlight the most notable patterns that can serve as background for researchers studying questions on education or labor markets in Qatar.

To carry out this overarching goal, the report has four specific objectives. First, we provide a detailed description of the methods used to collect and analyze the data. We describe the survey design, sampling frame, survey administration, post-administration data processing, and data analysis. We also report evidence on the degree to which the survey respondents resemble the population from which they were selected.

Second, we examine the educational plans and experiences of young Qataris. The survey collected information on the respondents' post-secondary schooling and their intention to pursue additional schooling in the future. We report on the type of schools respondents attended, the type of degree they pursued, and whether they successfully completed their degree program. Because the role of women in Qatari society is changing, these results are reported by gender to allow for comparisons between young men and women.

---

[2]   The most recent census was conducted in 2004; the one before that was conducted in 1997. The census collected basic information about the population of Qatar, including level of schooling, employment status, and household composition. Two labor-force surveys have also been conducted—one in 2001 and another in 2006. These surveys collect information included on the census questionnaire, as well as additional information about unemployment and type of job. The 2006 data had not been released at the time of this report.

Third, we summarize the data on early-career labor market experiences. We report descriptive statistics about the number and type of jobs respondents have had, as well as information about their current employment situation.

Fourth, we discuss young Qataris' attitudes toward school and work. Specifically, we tabulate the responses to questions that ask about the factors respondents feel are important to their choice of job and career, as well as their general attitudes toward school and work.

The report is organized as follows. Chapter Two discusses the methodological issues surrounding the survey design and administration. In Chapter Three, we discuss the survey tabulations. Chapter Four concludes the report and points to directions for future research. The appendix contains the survey instrument.

Methodology

This chapter has two purposes. The first is to describe in detail the methods that we used to collect the survey data. We begin by discussing the population of interest and the development of the questionnaire that we used to conduct the interviews. Next, we explain our approach to identifying and contacting potential respondents and describe the details of the survey administration. As we note below, the way we contacted respondents makes the representativeness of our sample an important issue. We therefore discuss how our survey respondents compare with the underlying population. The second is to describe the analytic methods we used to analyze the survey data.

Survey Target Population

In 2006, we conducted a cross-sectional survey of Qataris who had graduated from high school in 1998.[1] This group was selected so that we could collect information on the early-career experiences of young Qataris. When the survey was conducted, these individuals had been out of high school for eight years. In the intervening years, many students may have pursued post-secondary schooling, entered the labor market, and started families. Thus, by asking retrospective information on employment and schooling, we were able to obtain information on the nature of key transitions experienced by young adults in Qatar. In particular, we chose the eight-year time frame so that most students would have been able to complete their first stint in post-secondary education and make a decision about whether to enter the workforce.

Although asking retrospective questions allowed us to collect a great deal of information on a variety of important life events and transitions, retrospective survey data are problematic because respondents sometimes have difficulty correctly remembering all of what they are asked. This so-called recall bias is well known in the survey literature (Bound, Brown, and Mathiowetz, 2001) and may very well be present in our survey (although it is impossible to determine the extent and severity of such bias). In contrast, a longitudinal survey that asks respondents about events that happened very recently would have been less prone to recall bias. A longitudinal study would also have allowed the collection of even more detailed information on educational and labor market transitions. However, we had neither the resources nor the extended period of time needed to carry out this type of longitudinal survey. As we discuss

---

[1] As we describe below, our sampling universe included students who attended privately run schools and schools run by the government. It excluded anyone who did not graduate from high school. According to the 2004 census, about one-third of Qataris age 25–29 had not completed secondary school; a greater share of men (43 percent, compared with 26 percent for women) had not graduated.

in Chapter Four, policymakers should consider conducting a full-scale longitudinal survey to help inform the development of effective policies for young Qataris.

Survey Design

The survey was designed to collect information on the educational and employment experiences of young Qataris. The survey was organized into sections corresponding to these two subject areas. (The appendix contains the survey instrument.) Before addressing education and employment, however, the survey asked a series of questions on the respondent's family structure. These included marital status, year of marriage, and the number of children a respondent has.

The questions on work experience began with the respondent's current employment status and the number of jobs held since finishing high school. The rest of the questions on employment and work were skipped for those individuals who had never held a job. For those who had been employed at least once since high school, we then asked questions about the first and most recent job. These included the type of employer (e.g., government ministry, government enterprise), job title, and job duration.

We also gathered additional information on the qualifications and skills required in the respondent's most recent job. For instance, respondents were asked about the minimum level of education required for the job and the skills and attitudes necessary to do the job. Because interviews conducted by RAND researchers suggest that formal and informal job training is common in Qatar, we also collected information on any training the respondent had received to acquire skills identified as important for their most recent job.[2] We asked about the type of training (either on-the-job or at a formal training institution), where the training took place, and whether respondents were satisfied with their training.

Next, the survey asked a series of attitudinal questions.[3] The first set was about the factors seen as important in the choice of career.[4] The second set asked about the respondents' views toward school and work. These questions are one of the more interesting features of the data because they have no analog in any of the data collected by Qatar's national statistical agency.[5] Moreover, this information is helpful for understanding a number of crucial issues facing Qatar (and other Gulf State nations), such as why young people prefer public-sector employment and why the educational performance of men lags that of women.[6]

---

[2] Those interviews, with Qatari business, educational, and policy leaders, were conducted in December and February 2006 as part of the larger RAND study on post-secondary schooling in Qatar. See Stasz, Eide, and Martorell (2007) for additional information.

[3] We developed these items based on the information we were trying to collect and to test opinions that we had heard anecdotally from interviews with employers and policymakers. We did not adapt or adopt similar questions from other surveys.

[4] These questions were only asked of respondents who reported that they had at least one job since leaving high school.

[5] The Planning Council is the government agency that administers the census and the labor market surveys.

[6] As we show below, men are less likely to graduate from high school, and among high school graduates, are less likely to pursue post-secondary schooling.

The next section of the questionnaire covered educational and schooling. First, it asked about the respondents' high school field of study (i.e., their "major").[7] Respondents were then asked whether they were enrolled in school, their current level of education, and the highest level of schooling they expected to complete. For individuals who completed high school only, we asked about their reasons for not pursuing additional schooling.

Respondents who pursued additional schooling were then asked questions about their post-secondary schooling experiences. For the first and most recent higher educational institution attended, respondents indicated the location of the school, the degree they were pursuing, and whether they earned that degree. In addition, for the first school attended, respondents were also asked about their field of study or major and whether they received scholarship.

The final section of the survey was administered only to respondents who were not currently employed. Because these questions were part of a survey instrument that was separate from the "main" questionnaire, we refer to it as the "not employed supplement." This supplement was designed to acquire information on the experiences of individuals who chose not to work or who were unable to find a suitable job. It asked whether respondents were looking for work and, if so, what barriers they faced in doing to. For respondents who were not looking for work, we asked about the reasons why they chose not to be in the labor force.[8]

Sampling

We used Ministry of Education (MoE) administrative records to construct our sampling frame. Specifically, we sampled individuals from the registry of students who took the 1998 Secondary School Exit Exam. This registry includes both government-run schools and Independent schools, including the Religious Institute, the Industrial Institute, and private Arabic schools.[9] Although these records include students who failed the exit exam, we sampled only students who passed the exam so as to focus on individuals who graduated in 1998.[10]

Table 2.1 tabulates the number of exit exam takers by gender and passing status. Overall, 72 percent (1,881 out of 2,620) passed the test. These figures also underscore the consistent pattern that Qatari women outperform men in school. First, 56 percent of the test takers (1,480 out of 2,620) are women, indicating that men are more likely to drop out of high school before taking the exit exam. Second, conditional on taking the exit exam, women are much more likely to pass; the pass rate is 59 percent for men and over 81 percent for women.[11]

---

[7] In schools operated by the Ministry of Education, students select their secondary school field of study in 11th grade. The possible fields include "Science," "Literature, mathematics, and science," "French literature," "Industrial," "Commercial," and "Religious studies." Of these, "Science" is considered the most demanding field.

[8] This report does not discuss the responses to these questions because fewer than 30 respondents completed this part of the interview.

[9] The Religious Institute is no longer considered an Independent school.

[10] Students who earned a diploma by retaking and passing the exit exam at a later date were not included in our sampling frame.

[11] Passing status in Table 2.1 refers to *final* passing status, after any retests.

Table 2.1
Exit Exam Takers, by Passing Status and Gender

Gender	Fail	Pass	Total
Women	275	1,205	1,480
Men	464	676	1,140
Total	739	1,881	2,620

Our eventual goal was to survey 50 women and 50 men. An equal number of men and women were sampled so that we would have enough observations to do analyses by gender. We proceeded in two steps. We first drew a random sample of names from the exit exam registry. Sampling was done with replacement, so that each individual name had an equal probability of being selected. Using this approach, we drew a sample of 450 names; after deleting duplicates, we were left with a sample of 399. Of these, 146 were men and 253 were women. The second step involved contacting individuals on this list until we met the final sample size goal. Each name was given an identification number and randomly assigned to an interviewer on the research team of the same gender. Each interviewer had a target number of interviews to complete, based on his or her time availability during the data collection period. Each went down his or her list until the target number of interviews had been completed.

Survey Administration and Post-Administration Data Processing[12]

Interviewers administered the survey questionnaire to respondents over the telephone. A key challenge was successfully contacting the individuals selected for the survey. The first attempt was made by calling the phone number listed on the MoE exit exam database, which was generally the phone number of the parents' home as of 1998. In some cases, the person answering the interviewer's phone call suggested another number to try, which the interviewer used in any subsequent attempts to contact the potential respondent.

Interviewers made a maximum of three attempts to reach a name on their list. The attempts took place at different times of day and on at least two different days. The timing of the calls took into consideration local working hours, local weekends, and other social factors. If, after three attempts, the interviewer failed to reach the person or to conduct an interview, he or she documented those facts and moved on to the next name on the list.

Ultimately, we were able to complete 99 interviews (49 with women and 50 with men). All interviews were conducted in Arabic. Before administering the survey questions, the interviewer first explained to the respondent the purpose of the study and of the interview. Respondents were also informed that the data being collected could potentially be used by other RAND researchers but that their responses would be kept confidential (in the sense that their names would never be associated directly or indirectly with any information they provided). Respondents were also told that they were free to discontinue the interview at any point, although this did not occur.

Our plan to calculate survey response rates was to divide the number of completed surveys by the total number of individuals we tried to contact. Unfortunately, the forms that contained

---

[12] Hanine Salem provided much of the information contained in this section.

information on unsuccessful interview attempts for male respondents were lost. Therefore, we are not able to report a response rate for men. For women, we attempted to contact 169 women and completed 49 interviews. This resulted in a response rate of 29 percent.[13]

After conducting the interviews, research team members translated the write-in questionnaire items into English. The interview booklets were then photocopied and the copies were shipped to the RAND Santa Monica office. RAND's Survey Research Group (SRG) hand-entered the data according to data entry specifications we provided. We also provided SRG with an English version of the survey instrument. After SRG had completed data entry, a RAND programmer created SAS and STATA data files containing the raw data.

Sample Representativeness

The extent to which the survey respondents are representative of the underlying population is a crucial question when interpreting the results presented below and for assessing the appropriateness of these data for other purposes. Although we randomly sampled individuals from the exit exam registry, there are two reasons why our sample still might not be representative. First, since the final sample size is relatively small, we may have gotten "unlucky" and drawn a somewhat atypical group. A second possibility is that the survey respondents are systematically different from the individuals whom we sampled but were unable to interview.

One way to gauge the representativeness of the data is to compare the characteristics of individuals in our sample with those observed in the population used to draw the sample. Table 2.2 shows such a comparison for high school field of study.[14] The results suggest the distribution of field of study in our sample is reasonably similar to that in the population. Women who studied "Science" or "Literature, math, and science" are somewhat underrepresented, while women whose field of study was "French literature" are overrepresented.[15] For men the proportions of students specializing in a particular field are very similar in the sample and in the overall population. And for both men and women, a statistical test found no evidence that the distribution of field of study was different for the sample and for the population.[16]

---

[13] This figure includes nonresponse for all reasons, including inability to reach the potential respondent by phone. Despite this relatively low response rate, there is evidence to suggest that the characteristics of individuals in our sample are reasonably close to those of the underlying population. Moreover, research in the survey nonresponse literature indicates that sampling error is likely to swamp any systematic nonresponse bias in surveys with a small sample size, such as this one (Kessler, Little, and Groves, 1995).

[14] We focus on high school field of study because this information is available on the exit exam registry and was also recorded by the interviewers.

[15] The "Literature, math and science," "French literature," and "Science" fields have liberal arts curricula, but the latter emphasizes mathematics and the physical sciences. It focuses on coursework in science and mathematics and is generally considered the most academically rigorous field. "Commercial" and "Industrial" are mainly vocational degrees.

[16] Specifically, a chi-square test failed to reject the null hypothesis that distribution of field of study was the same in the sample and in the population (p-value for women = 0.26; p-value for men = 0.58).

Table 2.2
**Distribution of Field of Study, by Gender, 1998 Survey Respondents
and All 1998 High School Graduates (%)**

Field of Study	Women		Men	
	Population	Sample	Population	Sample
Science	30	24	38	40
Literature, math and science	52	47	52	50
French literature	18	29	2	0
Industrial	0	0	5	8
Commercial	0	0	2	2
Religious studies	0	0	0	0

SOURCE: Authors' calculations based on MoE exit exam database and 1998
cohort survey responses. N = 49 for women; N = 50 for men.

We also compared the educational attainment of survey respondents with figures available from the population census. Table 2.3 compares the fraction of individuals in the sample who report having more than a secondary degree and the fraction of Qataris age 25–29 who are listed in the 2004 census as having more than a secondary degree.[17] Strictly speaking, this is not an "apples-to-apples" comparison because not all the individuals in the 1998 cohort were between the ages of 25 and 29 at the time of the 2004 census, but this is the closest comparison that can be made. The results suggest that the women in the sample may be somewhat better educated than women in the overall population, with 79 percent of women in the sample having more than a secondary degree compared with 61 percent in the census. In contrast, the rate of post-secondary schooling for men is very close in the sample and in the census (51 percent in the sample and 46 percent in the census).

Table 2.3
**Those with More than a Secondary
Degree, by Gender, 1998 Survey and
2004 Census (%)**

Gender	2004 Census	Sample
Men	46	51
Women	61	79

SOURCE: Authors' calculations based on 1998
cohort survey responses and published
tabulations from the 2004 census. The census
figures refer to Qataris age 25–29 with at least
a secondary degree.

---

[17] The census figures in Table 2.3 refer only to individuals with at least a secondary degree so as to be comparable to the sampled population.

Analysis Approach

The analysis contained in this report uses basic descriptive statistics (such as sample means). Because the employment and educational patterns of men and women are very different and because this issue has received considerable attention from policymakers, all the results are presented by gender. In addition, some results are also presented by educational status. Where appropriate, we used standard statistical tests (e.g., t-test, chi-square test) to see whether differences across groups were statistically significant. Although we point out differences in the experiences of men and women, in keeping with the descriptive nature of the report, we generally do not discuss the reasons underlying such differences.

As noted previously, we attempted to sample an equal number of men and women, even though there are more women than men in the sampling universe.[18] For analysis purposes, the survey responses are weighted to adjust for the proportion of men and women in the population. Specifically, the sample weight for female respondents is equal to the ratio of the share of women in the population to the share of women in the sample: $(1{,}205/1{,}881)/(49/99) = 1.29$. The weight for men is $(676/1{,}881)/(50/99) = 0.71$. We used these weights whenever we generated estimates that pool data from male and female respondents.

---

[18] Note that the population in this case refers to all individuals in the MoE database who were seniors in 1998 and who passed the exit exam.

CHAPTER THREE

Survey Results

This chapter presents basic tabulations of the survey data. We begin by examining the family structure of respondents. Then we discuss their educational experiences. We examine the respondents' level of education, their post-secondary education experiences, and their plans for future study. Next, we turn to the early-career labor market experiences of recent high school graduates, for individuals who have worked and for those who have not worked. Finally, we present tabulations of the attitudinal questions on work and school.

Family Structure of Survey Respondents

Table 3.1 shows the tabulations of respondents' marital status and number of children. In our sample, 70 percent of men and roughly half the women reported being married (the male-female difference is statistically significant; $p = 0.04$).[1] These results are somewhat surprising since women generally marry at younger ages. For instance, according to the 2004 census, 50 percent of Qatari men age 25 to 29 are married compared with 62 percent of women. One possible reason for this discrepancy is that we sampled only individuals with at least a secondary degree. If age at first marriage is negatively related to education, we would expect a lower marriage rate in the sample compared with the population as a whole.[2] Another possibility is that the propensities to marry in the population and in the survey differ, which would indicate that on this dimension, at least, our sample might be somewhat nonrepresentative of the population at large.[3]

The results in Table 3.1 also show that almost 60 percent of the respondents had not yet had a child. Men were more likely than women to report having at least one child (56 percent compared with 33 percent; $p = 0.02$). This difference likely reflects the fact that women in the sample were also less likely than men to be married, and hence less likely to have begun having children.[4]

---

[1] Divorce is very rare; only one woman and no men indicated that they were divorced.

[2] The public census results include tabulations of marital status by education. Unfortunately, the census does not tabulate marital status by age and education. Thus, we cannot establish whether the marital rates in the sample are different from those among all individuals with at least a high school degree.

[3] This may be due to the fact that the parents' home phone number (as of 1998) was used to contact individuals who were selected from the exit exam registry. If married women are less likely to be living at home than single women, then they would be relatively more difficult to reach.

[4] We were not able to find statistics on out-of-wedlock childbearing in Qatar; the census reports only statistics on fertility among married women. However, given the country's conservative social norms, we suspect that it is rare.

Table 3.1
Marital Status and Number of Children, by Gender (%)

	Male	Female	Total
Marital status			
Single	30.0	49.0	42.2
Married	70.0	49.0	56.5
Divorced	0.0	2.0	1.3
Number of children			
0	44.2	66.7	59.3
1	25.6	16.7	19.6
2	20.9	10.4	13.9
3	7.0	6.3	6.5
4	2.3	0.0	0.8
Sample size	50	49	99

NOTE: We imputed zeros for the "number of children" variable for eight observations in which this information was missing but the respondent's marital status was "single."

Educational Experiences of Survey Respondents

We now turn to a discussion of the educational experiences of the respondents. As seen in Table 3.2, about half of both male and female respondents chose "Literature, mathematics, and science" as their high school major field. The major field for most of the remaining males was "Science" (40 percent compared with 24 percent for females; p = 0.10).[5] None of the males decided to pursue "French literature," which was the second most frequent choice among females (29 percent). None of the females and only a handful of males chose "Industrial" or "Commercial" as a major field.

Table 3.3 shows the respondents' level of educational attainment as of the survey. Overall, 31 percent of respondents indicate that they have not completed any schooling beyond secondary. These figures also show that Qatari women outperformed men in gaining post-

Table 3.2
Major Field of Study in High School, by Gender (%)

Major Field	Male	Female	Total
Science	40.0	24.5	30.1
Literature, mathematics, and science	50.0	46.9	48.0
French literature	0.0	28.6	18.3
Industrial	8.0	0.0	2.9
Commercial	2.0	0.0	0.7
Sample size	50	49	99

[5] The "Literature, mathematics, and science" field is similar to a liberal arts curriculum. In contrast, "Science" has a more technical focus.

Table 3.3
Current Level of Education, by Gender (%)

Education Level	Male	Female	Total
Secondary	48.0	20.8	30.7
Post-secondary diploma	16.0	8.3	11.1
University/bachelor's degree	30.0	70.8	56.0
Higher diploma	4.0	0.0	1.5
Other	2.0	0.0	0.7
Sample size	50	48	98

secondary degrees. Only about half of men have completed a post-secondary degree compared with almost 80 percent of women (p < 0.01). Similarly, females were much more likely than males to have earned a bachelor's degree or higher (71 percent compared with 34 percent; p < 0.01).

Table 3.4 reports the number of post-secondary institutions that respondents have attended. Eighty-one percent of respondents in our sample have been enrolled in at least one post-secondary program. Although, consistent with the results in Table 3.3, a greater fraction of women than men report having pursued post-secondary studies (85 percent compared with 74 percent), the sample size is not sufficient for this difference to be statistically significant (p = 0.16). The table also reveals that women are less likely to attend multiple post-secondary institutions. Most women (83 percent) attended exactly one post-secondary institution compared with about one half of male respondents (p < 0.01).

We then asked respondents to indicate the degree pursued at the first post-secondary institution they attended. Responses are tabulated in Table 3.5 by gender and by whether or not the degree was received (note that Table 3.5 includes only respondents who reported having attended at least one post-secondary institution). Among those who pursued post-secondary schooling, 80 percent attended a university-level degree program. Twelve percent continued post-secondary study at lower-level diploma-granting programs. Four percent reported they sought a post-graduate degree. This may be due to misreporting (perhaps because they misinterpreted the question) or because their program was a joint bachelor-master's degree program.

These numbers again show higher post-secondary education achievement among Qatari females compared with Qatari males. More than 90 percent of female respondents reported pursuing at least a bachelor's degree. In contrast, only about two-thirds of men pursued at least a bachelor's degree. Interestingly, the share of those who studied at the university level

Table 3.4
Number of Post-Secondary Schools Attended, by Gender (%)

Number of Schools	Male	Female	Total
None	26.0	14.6	18.7
One	50.0	83.3	71.2
More than one	24.0	2.1	10.1
Sample size	50	48	98

Table 3.5
Respondents Studying for a Degree at Their First Post-Secondary Institution (%)

| Degree | Gender | | Degree Completion | | |
	Male	Female	Degree Completed	Degree Not Completed	Total
Diploma	21.1	7.3	11.0	14.9	12.0
University	65.8	87.8	84.3	67.9	80.4
Higher diploma	2.6	0.0	1.2	0.0	0.9
Master's degree	0.0	4.9	0.0	13.5	3.2
Other	10.5	0.0	3.5	3.7	3.6
Sample size	38	41	57	22	79

was higher among those who completed the degree than that among the respondents who did not complete the degree—84 percent compared with 68 percent—although this difference is not statistically significant (p = 0.16). Overall, 72 percent of individuals who went on for post-secondary study completed their degree.[6]

We also examined fields of study pursued at the first post-secondary institution (see Table 3.6) and found a number of interesting differences between men and women. For men, "Engineering" was the most popular field (20 percent) followed by "Computers, math, and science" (17 percent), "Law" (11 percent), and "Business administration" (11 percent). In contrast, none of the women studied "Engineering" or "Law." Women were concentrated in fields that no men pursued, such as "Humanities, arts, and literature" (26 percent) or "Education" (20 percent). However, it should be borne in mind that the small sample sizes make it difficult to make firm inferences about the distribution of major field of study.

Regarding the type of the first post-secondary school, two-thirds of respondents who had ever studied in post-secondary education institutions initially attended a four-year school (Table 3.6). The institution type for most of the remaining respondents fell into the "other" category. However, Table 3.5 shows that more than two-thirds of the respondents (nearly 84 percent) indicated that they initially pursued a bachelor's (or higher) degree. Thus, the true fraction attending a four-year institution may be higher than what is reported in Table 3.6.[7]

Table 3.7 shows degree completion status at the first post-secondary school by gender. Overall, 76 percent of the respondents received the degrees being pursued. Again, female respondents outperformed males on this measure of post-secondary persistence—85 percent of them received the degrees compared with 58 percent of males. This difference is statistically significant (p < 0.01).

We also asked respondents to indicate the location of their first post-secondary school (Table 3.8). Almost one-third of males went abroad for study while none of the females did. This difference may be attributable to tradition and family responsibilities that preclude study abroad for some women.

---

[6]   A large majority of respondents initially pursued a university degree. Of these individuals, 76 percent ended up completing the degree.

[7]   The discrepancy may be due to misreporting. Interviewees may not have understood the distinction that we were trying to make between types of institution, which led to them naming some third type of institution that may actually be a standard four-year institution.

Table 3.6
Major Field of Study in the First Post-Secondary Institution (%)

Major Field	Gender		School Type			
	Male	Female	Vocational, Trade, Business	Four-Year Institution	Other	Total
Business administration	11.4	12.8	50.0	11.4	10.2	12.4
Art and design	2.9	5.1	0.0	6.4	0.0	4.4
Law	11.4	0.0	0.0	4.1	3.4	3.8
Education	0.0	20.5	0.0	12.5	18.5	13.7
Computers, math, and science	17.1	10.3	0.0	11.9	15.7	12.5
Sharia/Islamic studies	2.9	5.1	0.0	6.4	0.0	4.4
Engineering	20.0	0.0	0.0	4.1	13.5	6.6
Social science	8.6	5.1	0.0	9.1	0.0	6.3
Humanities, arts, literature	0.0	25.6	0.0	20.0	12.3	17.2
Information systems and library	2.9	5.1	0.0	6.4	0.0	4.4
Other	22.9	10.3	50.0	7.8	26.5	14.4
Sample size	35	39	2	49	23	74

Table 3.7
Degree Completion at First Post-Secondary School, by Gender (%)

Degree Completion Status	Male	Female	Total
Received	57.9	85.4	76.1
Not received	42.1	14.6	23.9
Sample size	38	41	79

Table 3.8
Location of the First Post-Secondary School, by Gender (%)

Location	Male	Female	Total
Qatar	67.6	100.0	89.2
Abroad	32.4	0.0	10.8
Sample size	37	41	78

Labor Force Experiences of Survey Respondents

This section presents the tabulations of the survey questions on work and employment experiences. We begin with summary measures of respondents' attachment to the labor force, such as their current labor force status and whether they have ever held a job. Next, for individuals who are currently working, we examine the characteristics of their job: how they found out about it, the type of organization that employs them, and the skills and training associated with the job. Finally, we present the results for the attitudinal questions on work and school.

Labor Force Participation and Job Search Methods

The upper part of Table 3.9 shows the average labor force status for sample members by gender. Labor force attachment is very high for men, the vast majority of whom (88 percent) were employed at the time of the survey. Moreover, almost all men were in the labor force, with only 4 percent (2 individuals) reporting that they were not employed and not looking for a job. The implied unemployment rate (the percentage of unemployed individuals among those who either have a job or are looking for work) is 8.3 percent. Although this rate suggests that a nontrivial segment of young Qataris have trouble finding employment, it is in line with that found in the United States and Europe.[8]

In contrast, women have much lower labor force participation rates and are much less likely to be working. As of the survey date, just over half of female respondents (54 percent) were employed and 23 percent were out of the labor force altogether (i.e., not working and not looking for work). Given the traditional nature of gender roles in Qatar (Winckler, 2000), these results are not surprising. What is interesting, however, is that the unemployment rate is quite high (23 percent).[9] One possible reason why unemployment is so prevalent among women is that there is a shortage of jobs where the work environment allows women to adhere to their cultural and religious traditions. For instance, consider teaching. Teaching is a desirable occupation for many women because female teachers generally have limited interactions with adult men (as we show below, very few Qatari men are teachers; boys' schools are primarily staffed by expatriate men) and teaching does not require long work hours that would limit the time spent with one's family.[10] To the extent that the number of women interested in working as teachers outstrips the available teaching positions, high female unemployment rates will be the result.

Table 3.9 also shows the number of jobs individuals have held in the eight years since finishing high school. Interestingly, relatively few individuals held more than one job (28 percent

Table 3.9
Labor Force Status and Cumulative Number of Jobs Held Since High School, by Gender (%)

	Male	Female	Total
Labor force status			
Employed	88.0	54.2	66.5
Not employed, looking for a job	8.0	22.9	17.5
Not employed, not looking for a job	4.0	22.9	16.0
Number of jobs since finishing high school			
None	6.0	42.9	29.6
One	66.0	44.9	52.5
Two and more	28.0	12.2	17.9
Sample size	50	49	99

[8]   Unemployment in the United States among 25- to 29-year-old men in 2006 was 5 percent (Bureau of Labor Statistics, 2007). In Germany, the overall unemployment rate in July 2006 among men was 8.5 percent, and it was 18 percent among men younger than 25 (Statistisches Bundesamt Deutschland, 2007).

[9]   The unemployment rate among women in the 2001 Labor Force Survey is 27 percent (Planning Council, 2002).

[10]   Stasz, Eide, and Martorell (2007) report that 44 percent of currently employed women work as teachers.

for men and 12 percent for women). In contrast, Americans hold an average of 6.8 jobs between the ages of 18 and 25 (Bureau of Labor Statistics, 2006).[11] Thus, it appears that career changes are somewhat uncommon in Qatar, at least relative to what is seen in the United States.

An interesting feature of these data is the information on how respondents found out about their most recent job (Table 3.10). To the extent that encouraging private-sector work is a policy goal, it is important to understand how relatively new entrants into the labor force learn about available jobs. The results indicate that the civil-service job placement service is the most important avenue for women to learn about jobs. In contrast, "other" is the most common source of job information for men.[12] For both men and women, information provided at their school or by friends was also used. Perhaps surprisingly, family members are a relatively unimportant source of information for both men and women, although "family" and "friends" together are the source of information about the current job for about 25 percent of respondents.

Occupation and Employer Type

We now turn to an examination of the characteristics of the most recent job for respondents who indicated that they were currently employed.[13] The results in Table 3.11 clearly show that an overwhelming majority of individuals in our sample were employed by a government ministry or in a government-owned corporation (such as Qatar Petroleum). Almost no one worked in the private sector; in our sample, no women did. This is consistent with evidence from the

Table 3.10
Source of Information About Current Job, by Gender (%)

Sources of Information	Male	Female	Total
Civil-service job placement	6.8	46.2	27.2
Nongovernmental job placement service	0.0	3.9	2.0
School attended	13.6	15.4	14.5
Family	9.1	7.7	8.4
Friends	13.6	19.2	16.5
Business associate	0.0	3.9	2.0
Newspapers or television	2.3	7.7	5.1
Other sources	63.6	3.9	32.7
Sample size	44	25	69

---

[11] This figure is based on a longitudinal study of individuals who were age 14 to 21 in 1979.

[12] It is not clear how to interpret this result. Although not one of the closed-ended options on the questionnaire, many men simply told the interviewer that they applied directly to the job.

[13] Similar results were found when we included the six respondents who reported ever having a job but who are not currently working. These individuals were excluded in order to focus on respondents who were actively engaged in the labor market at the time of the survey. We also focus on the most recent job because few respondents (N = 24) reported any information about their first job. Furthermore, the questionnaire contains relatively few items about the first job.

Table 3.11
Distribution of Employer Types, by Gender (%)

Type of Organization	Male	Female	Total
Government	48.8	72.0	60.7
Government-owned	41.9	28.0	34.7
Private	2.3	0.0	1.1
Other	7.0	0.0	3.4
Sample size	43	25	68

census, which also indicates very low employment rates in the private sector (Planning Council, 2005). One interesting pattern is that women tend to be employed in government ministries while men are more evenly distributed between employment in a ministry or in a company owned by the government (72 percent of women work for a ministry compared with 49 percent of men; $p = 0.06$). This partly reflects the fact that many women work as teachers and are therefore civil servants employed by the Ministry of Education.

The survey also collected information about the respondent's occupation by asking for the job title of the most recent job. To organize the occupation data, we recoded the self-reported job titles into categories used by the Planning Council in publicly released tabulations of census data. Specifically, the Planning Council used the International Standard Classification of Occupations–88 (ISCO-88) to group occupations, and we used the same scheme to guide the mapping from written-in job title to occupation category.[14] However, there were a few occupations in which many respondents worked; they are identified separately in Table 3.12. These are "Associate professional," "Military/police," and "Teacher." Also, we excluded several groups used by the Planning Council because no respondents worked in those occupations (e.g., agricultural worker). To understand how these mappings were done, Table 3.12 shows each of the occupational categories we used and two examples of the unedited job titles that were assigned to each group.

Table 3.12
Occupational Category and Examples of Unedited Job Title

Occupation Category	Unedited Job Title
Associate professional	"Help desk administrator," "Legal researcher"
Clerk	"Administration (assistant)," "Administrative staff data entry"
Elementary	"Security supervisor," "Security man"
Legislator/senior officer/manager	"Senior accountant," "Chairman of the board"
Military or police	"Police officer," "Air force pilot"
Operator	"Operator," "Senior operator"
Professional	"Accounting specialist," "Editor"
Service worker	"Store keeper"
Teacher	"Teacher," "Art teacher"
Technician	"Technician I," "Mechanical technician"

---

[14] The International Labour Organization's Web site describes the ISCO-88 classification system. See International Labour Organization (2004).

Using this classification scheme, Table 3.13 tabulates the occupational distribution in the sample. Several interesting patterns emerge. First, almost half of the currently employed female respondents worked as teachers, while only one male respondent did. Second, "Military or police" was the second most common occupational category for men (18 percent), but no women worked in this field. Third, the other occupational groupings do not show large gender differences (none is statistically significant). On first glance, this might seem strange considering that women tend to complete more schooling and hence would be expected to concentrate in occupations that require higher levels of education. However, this pattern is caused by separating the "Teacher" and "Professional" categories. If these are combined (as they would be according to ISCO-88), women substantially outnumber men in professional occupations.

Education and Skills Needed for Current Job

We now examine the educational credentials and skills respondents needed for their jobs. Note this is based on *self-reported* information about credentials and skills needed, not on an outside source or agency. Table 3.14 shows that women are more likely than men to work in a job that requires an advanced degree. More than half (56) of currently employed women work in a job that requires a university diploma, while only 30 percent of men do ($p = 0.03$). Over half of men work in jobs that require no more than a secondary school diploma, compared with 20 percent of women.

Table 3.13
Occupation Category, by Gender (%)

Occupation	Male	Female	Total
Associate professional	13.3	11.1	12.2
Clerk	15.6	18.5	17.1
Elementary	4.4	0.0	2.1
Legislator or senior officer	4.4	3.8	4.1
Military or police	17.8	0.0	8.5
Operator	8.9	0.0	4.3
Professional	20.0	14.8	17.3
Service worker	2.2	0.0	1.1
Teacher	4.4	44.4	25.3
Technician	8.9	7.4	8.1
Sample size	45	27	72

Table 3.14
Minimum Level of Education Needed to Get Current Job, by Gender (%)

Education Level	Male	Female	Total
Less than secondary school	11.6	8.0	9.8
Secondary school	41.9	12.0	26.5
Post-secondary diploma	16.3	24.0	20.3
University degree	30.2	56.0	43.5
Sample size	43	25	68

These results are consistent with the educational gender gap discussed in Chapter Two. Pushing this notion further, an interesting question is whether sample respondents have just enough education for their current job or whether they are overeducated in the sense that they have more education than their current job requires. Table 3.15 indicates that the educational attainment of 26 percent of male and 33 percent of female respondents exceeds that required by their job (the male-female difference is not statistically significant). Although this may indicate that recent labor market entrants might face some underemployment, these data do not allow us to determine whether this condition will diminish as the respondents gain work experience and earn promotions to more-senior positions.

Another way to gain insight about the respondents' job requirements is to examine the skills they claimed were most important in their current job.[15] The survey asked respondents whether they used a series of skills. Table 3.16 shows that interpersonal interactions were considered important: Almost all individuals in the sample indicated that giving and taking orders and working in a team were important features of their jobs (since members of the sample are fairly young, it is surprising that so many respondents said that giving directions was an important job skill). Most respondents also said that they used a foreign language and their reading and writing skills, indicating the high value of communication skills. Although basic problem-solving, computer, and math skills were widely used, specialized technical or computer skills were less important. Interestingly, Table 3.16 shows few notable differences between men and women, which is somewhat surprising given the gender differential in education. The largest difference is for use of a foreign language, which was cited by almost all men (93 percent) but only about two-thirds of women ($p = 0.03$).

Training

Formal job training is widespread in Qatar (Planning Council, 2005), and the survey asked several questions about the training respondents received.[16] Table 3.17 confirms that job training participation rates are indeed high. Two-thirds of men and nearly half of currently employed

**Table 3.15
Correspondence of Education and Job Requirements, by Gender (%)**

Correspondence	Male	Female	Total
Overeducated	26.2	33.3	29.8
Just enough education	66.7	62.5	64.5
Undereducated	7.1	4.2	5.6
Sample size	44	26	70

---

[15] The survey included a list of potential skills, and asked respondents whether each skill was one of the most important needed to do the current job.

[16] As discussed in Stasz, Eide, and Martorell (2007), there are myriad training providers in Qatar, and training is provided by organizations in all sectors of the economy including the government, government-owned companies, and non-government organizations (both for-profit and not-for-profit).

Table 3.16
Skills That Are Most Important to the Current Job, by Gender (%)

Skill Category	Male	Female	Total
Basic math	72.7	57.7	64.9
Reading and writing	88.6	84.6	86.6
Advanced math	20.5	23.1	21.8
Basic computer skills	75.0	61.5	68.0
Advanced computer skills	22.7	23.1	22.9
Specific technology or equipment	54.6	34.6	44.2
To work in a team	95.5	76.9	85.9
Communicate with outside customers	75.0	73.1	74.0
English or other foreign language	93.2	65.4	78.8
To solve problems	88.6	76.9	82.6
Follow directions from a supervisor	95.5	92.3	93.8
To give directions to other people	86.4	80.8	83.5
Sample size	44	25	69

women indicated that they received training for the skills that they indicated were important for their job (the male-female difference is marginally statistically significant; p = 0.12). This is noteworthy since it indicates that substantial human capital investments in Qatar occur outside of formal schooling.[17]

Table 3.18 tabulates training by whether the respondent works for a government ministry or for a government-owned company. Training is more common among respondents who are employed by a government-owned corporation than in a ministry (p = 0.03), with over three-quarters of respondents who work at a government company indicating that they received training. This differential is consistent with the view that employment in a ministry is less skill-intensive than work in a government enterprise, although this fact alone does not prove that conjecture.[18]

Table 3.17
Respondents Receiving Formal Job Training to Learn Skills for Current Job, by Gender (%)

Formal Training Received	Male	Female	Total
Yes	67.4	48.0	57.5
No	32.6	52.0	42.6
Sample size	44	25	69

[17] On the other hand, the recent Planning Council (2005) study indicates that much of the training that takes place in Qatar is not very intensive.

[18] The Ministry of Civil Service and Housing provides the bulk of training for employees in government jobs. The most popular training programs are management programs, followed by finance and information technology. In contrast, training provided by government corporations such as Qatar Petroleum includes training for clerical and technical jobs, as well as English-language training (Stasz, Eide, and Martorell, 2007).

Table 3.18
Formal Training by Employer Type, by Gender (%)

Formal Training Received	Type of Employer		Total
	Government	Government-Owned	
Yes	48.8	75.2	58.5
No	51.2	24.9	41.5
Sample size	38	25	63

Experiences of Not-Employed Respondents

We conclude this section by discussing the responses to the survey supplement for not-employed respondents. Since most respondents were employed, this supplement was administered only to 28 individuals (22 females and 6 males). As a consequence of the relatively small number of respondents, strong conclusions should not be drawn from these results, and we report only pooled tabulations rather than results by gender.

Among the not-employed respondents, just over half (15 out of 28) indicated that they were actively seeking work. Job-seekers were then asked about the types of jobs they were considering. The only desired employers were government (13 out of 15 respondents, 84 percent) and government-owned organizations (7 out of 15, 43 percent). None of the respondents favored the other types of employers (see Table 3.19).[19]

To better understand the barriers to finding employment, respondents who were looking for employment were asked whether they felt a series of potential factors were impeding their ability to find a job. Table 3.20 shows that competition for jobs is seen as an important barrier by most, with 69 percent of respondents indicating that there were too few job openings and 73 percent saying that competition for jobs is a reason for not being able to find work. Fewer than half of those respondents indicated that any of the other factors were reasons for not being able to find work.

We also tried to understand the reasons why respondents who were not seeking work chose not to do so. The most important factor was family responsibilities. About half (6 of 13) of the respondents attributed their decisions to this factor. One-third (4 of 13) of the respondents just did not enjoy work, and about one-quarter (3 of 13) said that lack of education or training influenced their decision (see Table 3.21).

Table 3.19
**Type of Desired Employer for Those
Who Have Never Worked**

Desired Employer	%
Government	84
Government-owned organization	43
Other	0
Sample size	15

---

[19] Note that the percentages in Table 3.19 are calculated using sample weights.

Table 3.20
Reasons for Not Being Able to Find Work

Reason	%
Not enough job openings	69
Available jobs pay too little	27
Do not have skills for available jobs	8
Too many hours to work required at available jobs	30
Social position of available jobs unacceptable	39
High competition for jobs I am looking for	73
Lack of family and/or personal connections	16
Child care not available	8
Sample size	15

Table 3.21
Reasons for Not Looking for Work

Reason	%
Family responsibilities	49.6
Health problems prevent work	0.0
Societal/parental expectations	16.5
Don't enjoy work	33.1
Other activities more lucrative	8.3
Don't have the education or training I need	24.8
Other reasons	25.6
Sample size	13

Finally, we asked respondents whether they were interested in pursuing additional education or training to acquire skills that would be helpful for finding a job. Eighty percent (16 out of 20) of respondents who indicated they were either seeking employment or who felt that they might be interested in seeking employment if they possessed better skills indicated that they did plan to pursue additional training or education.[20] Despite the small sample size, this result suggests that there may be demand on the part of young adults who have completed their initial stint in school for programs that offer opportunities to acquire new skills. When asked what kind of training or educational opportunity they would like to pursue, about two-thirds (11 out of 16) indicated they were most interested in formal schooling, while a little less than half reported being interested in formal job training (6 out of 11) or in a foreign language or computer training program (7 out of 11).[21]

---

[20] This question was asked of individuals who were looking for a job or who indicated that they would be more likely to work if they had better training and education.

[21] Note that respondents could indicate interest in pursuing more than one form of training or education.

Attitudes About Choice of Career, Schoool, and Work

We conclude this chapter by discussing the responses to the survey's two attitudinal questions, starting with the factors that are important to the choice of career (see Table 3.22).[22] Understanding the determinants of career choice and job is critical if policymakers want to successfully encourage young Qataris to pursue employment opportunities outside the public sector. For each factor, respondents were asked to indicate how important each factor was to them on a four-point scale (with "4" being extremely important and "1" denoting not important). Table 3.22 reports the mean of the four-point scale and the implied rank orderings. The most important factor for both men and women is that a job "makes me feel respected."[23] Job security, opportunities for career advancement, and the chance to contribute to society are also relatively important for men and women.

One interesting pattern is that factors related to financial compensation (e.g., salary, retirement benefits) are ranked in the middle of the factors the survey asked about. If these responses accurately depict determinants of job choice, policies that offer monetary rewards for participating in the private sector might actually be less effective than policies that make private-sector employment more prestigious and less volatile (in terms of job security).[24]

Although men and women tend to view the same factors as important or unimportant, several important differences exist. Men tend to place more importance on monetary compensation. For instance, salary is the seventh most important factor for men and has an average ranking score of 3, while it is the fifteenth most important factor for women, with only a mean ranking of 2.7 ($p < 0.01$).[25] Another example is "friendly colleagues," which is the fourth most important factor for women but only the eleventh most important for men (the mean difference in the importance scale is very small, however).

As expected, a single-gender work environment is more important for women than men. For women, it has an average ranking of 2.9, while for men it ranks 1.8 ($p < 0.01$). More than two-thirds of women (68 percent) indicated that they felt that a single-gender environment is "extremely" or "very important." Looked at from a different angle, however, it is somewhat surprising that nearly one-third of female respondents indicated that a single-gender environment was only "somewhat important" or not important at all. Similarly, a single-gender environment was only the thirteenth most important factor for women. Although we do not have longitudinal data to test this claim directly, this result hints at the possibility that attitudes toward gender roles in Qatar are changing.

In the second attitudinal question, respondents were asked to state the level of their agreement with a series of statements pertaining to school and work on a four-point scale, with

---

[22] In contrast to the results presented for the most-recent job, the results in Table 3.22 include both individuals who indicated that they had ever worked for pay since high school and individuals with missing information on the number of jobs since high school.

[23] This result is consistent with sociological research showing that status and hierarchy are very important in Arab societies (Gingrich, 1995).

[24] It is, of course, difficult to envision ways of making private-sector employment more secure without its becoming much like public-sector work is today.

[25] In the discussion of Table 3.22, p-values are for the comparison of average rankings, not rank-orderings.

Table 3.22
Importance of Job Characteristics to Choice of Job or Career

Characteristic	Male			Female			Total		
	Mean	Std. Err.	Rank	Mean	Std. Err.	Rank	Mean	Std. Err.	Rank
Makes me feel respected and appreciated	3.77	0.07	1	3.82	0.07	1	3.79	0.05	1
Job security	3.53	0.09	4	3.68	0.10	2	3.61	0.07	2
Opportunities for career advancement	3.72	0.07	2	3.32	0.14	6	3.51	0.08	3
Make a contribution to society	3.53	0.10	5	3.43	0.16	3	3.48	0.09	4
Opportunity to get more training	3.55	0.09	3	3.39	0.13	5	3.47	0.08	5
Friendly colleagues	3.30	0.13	11	3.43	0.14	4	3.37	0.09	6
Allows time to be with family	3.37	0.12	9	3.11	0.17	9	3.23	0.10	7
Interesting work	3.26	0.12	12	3.18	0.15	8	3.22	0.09	8
Challenging work	3.17	0.14	13	3.04	0.19	10	3.10	0.12	9
Salary	3.43	0.09	7	2.71	0.18	15	3.06	0.10	10
Vacations	2.81	0.12	16	3.25	0.18	7	3.04	0.11	11
Retirement benefits	3.37	0.11	8	2.62	0.17	17	2.99	0.11	12
Other benefits	3.34	0.11	10	2.64	0.16	16	2.98	0.10	13
Housing benefits	3.47	0.11	6	2.48	0.19	18	2.96	0.12	14
Prestige	2.85	0.17	15	2.93	0.19	12	2.89	0.12	15
Not expected to work long hours	2.74	0.17	17	2.96	0.17	11	2.86	0.12	16
Bonuses	2.89	0.13	14	2.82	0.18	14	2.85	0.11	17
Women-only work environment	1.84	0.17	18	2.86	0.21	13	2.39	0.14	18
Mixed-gender work environment	1.42	0.11	19	1.39	0.13	19	1.41	0.08	19
Sample size		47			28			75	

NOTE: Means refer to average importance, where importance is measured using a four-point scale (1 = not important, 2 = somewhat important, 3 = very important, and 4 = extremely important).

"1" indicating complete disagreement and "4" complete agreement.[26] Table 3.23 shows that respondents uniformly agree on the importance of getting a good education. Similarly, over 80 percent of respondents felt that "people think better of you if you have a university degree." Despite the importance of education, only two-thirds of respondents agreed that getting good grades helps to get a better job. This suggests that the level of schooling may be more important than actual performance or knowledge gained in school. It is also interesting to note that only about one-third of the sample members agreed with the view that it was necessary to go abroad to receive the best education, the lowest rate of agreement with any of the statements. This result is interesting, especially considering the perception that Qatar's educational offerings are of relatively low quality (Stasz, Eide, and Martorell, 2007). It may be that young Qataris think

---

[26] All respondents were asked this question, and their answers are tabulated here. Restricting the sample to those who are currently employed yields similar results.

Table 3.23
Views Toward School and Work, by Gender (%)

| | Somewhat or Completely Agree | | |
Statement	Male	Female	Total
It is important to get a good education	98.0	100.0	99.3
Getting good grades at school helps you get a better job	76.0	63.3	67.8
You have to go abroad to get the best education	36.0	34.7	35.2
People think better of you if you have a university degree	84.0	81.6	82.5
There should be more jobs open to women	75.0	95.8	88.4
The best jobs in Qatar are in the government	32.0	65.3	53.3
People who study a technical field (e.g., engineering) can get a higher paying job	86.0	67.3	74.1
Work is harder in private companies than in government jobs	80.0	67.3	71.9
To get a good job, who you know is more important than what you know	68.0	51.0	57.1
Sample size	50	49	99

NOTE: Respondents could agree with more than one statement.

local offerings are better than they are. Alternatively, the introduction of world-class institutions in Education City may have changed perceptions about the need to go abroad.

An important result is that a large majority (72 percent) indicated that they felt work is harder in private companies than in government jobs. This is consistent with the belief expressed by employers that Qatari workers are reluctant to work outside the government sector because working conditions are too demanding (Stasz, Eide, and Martorell, 2007). It also underscores the difficulty policymakers might have if they hope to lure young Qataris out of government-sector employment.

A number of interesting patterns emerge when examining the responses by gender. A large majority of respondents agreed that more jobs should be open to women, although more women than men felt that way (96 percent compared with 75 percent; $p < 0.01$). Women were also more likely to agree that the best jobs in Qatar are in the government (65 percent compared with 32 percent; $p < 0.01$), which is consistent with the larger share of women working in government schools or ministries. Finally, men are more likely to agree that studying a technical field can help get a higher-paying job (86 percent compared with 67 percent; $p = 0.03$). One explanation for this pattern is that women may feel that investments in technical training yield little payoff because some jobs are not open to them, but we do not have the data to directly test that hypothesis.

CHAPTER FOUR

Summary and Conclusions

This report describes a small-scale survey of recent Qatari high school graduates. The survey was designed to help policymakers understand: (1) the types of educational experiences high school graduates have, (2) early-career labor market experiences of high school graduates, and (3) attitudes toward school and work. We now briefly summarize the tabulations from this survey here.

Educational Experiences

- Four-fifths of respondents pursued some post-secondary schooling, and two-thirds reported holding a post-secondary degree.
- Sharp gender differences in schooling attainment were found; only half of men had a post-secondary degree compared with 80 percent of women.
- Men and women also differed in post-secondary field. For instance, "Education" and "Humanities, arts, and literature" were exclusively pursued by women.
- One-third of men studied abroad, compared with no female respondents.

Labor Market Experiences

- Two-thirds of respondents were employed at the time of the survey.
- Employment rates were much higher among men (88 percent) than among women (54 percent).
- Virtually all respondents were employed by the government or by a government-owned corporation (such as Qatar Petroleum).
- Foreign-language skills, especially among men, were cited as important for the respondents' current job.

Attitudes Toward School and Work

- Being made to feel respected was the most important job characteristic for both men and women.

- Respondents held fairly progressive views toward women in the workforce. Eighty-eight percent of all respondents and 75 percent of men thought more jobs should be open to women.

Looking more broadly, this report also suggests a sampling and survey strategy that might be used in other contexts where identifying and contacting the target population is difficult. However, it is important to recognize some inherent limitations that arise because of the nature of the survey and our sampling approach. The first concerns the small size of the sample. Due to resource constraints, we were able to conduct only 99 interviews. Although this small survey is a unique resource for understanding the experiences of young adults in Qatar, it should be recognized that a number of analyses are not practical with such a small sample. For instance, for policymakers trying to determine whether there is a need for additional educational offerings (perhaps targeted at students who did not pursue post-secondary studies, such as a community college), it would be extremely helpful to understand the extent of skill deficiencies not only by gender but also by level of education and type of job. Our sample simply is not large enough to carry out this sort of detailed cross-tabulation. Future efforts to collect a larger sample would allow useful analyses such as this one to be done.

Second, the strategy we used to contact individuals might have introduced biases that make the sample unrepresentative of the underlying population of high school graduates from which we drew our sample. We explored this possibility and did not find compelling evidence of such biases, but ultimately we cannot rule it out entirely. Finally, these results naturally pertain only to the specific population we sampled and are not informative about other subgroups that might be of particular interest. For instance, we did not sample students who dropped out of high school, a group which some fear has been growing recently (Planning Council, 2005).

These limitations point to several directions for future research. One would be to conduct larger surveys that could enable, for instance, a comparison of the jobs held by men and women who complete university degrees. A larger sample would have obvious analytic advantages for such a comparison. Another would be to conduct surveys of other populations, such as secondary school dropouts.

One interesting possibility would be to conduct a longitudinal study that follows students for several years after completing high school. This study would allow researchers to better understand the determinants of students' decisions as they enter the workforce or pursue additional schooling.

Such a study could be very informative for policymakers. For example, if several successive cohorts of college graduates with a particular major field of study experience low unemployment rates and high wages, it would be a signal that students specializing in that area are in high demand and that admissions to that major ought to be increased. In the opposite case—i.e., when graduates from particular fields experience difficulties securing jobs, a policy recommendation would be to reduce investments in that field. Alternatively, such a finding might indicate the need for a change in the curriculum to target the needs of the labor market more effectively. In addition, the information about what drives behavior of Qatari youth (in particular, their educational and labor market decisions) would be very helpful for policymakers trying to understand how behavior might be changed. As new social and political changes are introduced, this knowledge will likely become more useful.

Conceivably, a longitudinal survey could be useful for jobseekers. By showing trajectories of individuals who have made a variety of decisions, especially those similar to the ones they themselves contemplate, a longitudinal survey could help Qataris make effective decisions about their future jobs.

It could also be useful to conduct regular surveys of employers. These would collect information about employer perceptions of the skills of their employees and about the occupations they find difficult to fill because of a shortage of skilled applicants interested in the job. To obtain a more comprehensive picture, employers' opinions could be accompanied by market signals, such as the wages and other benefits they pay workers; together, these data could provide an indication of where more investment is needed. An employer survey would also be interesting because of all the anecdotal evidence about their views. Stasz, Eide, and Martorell (2007) conducted informal interviews for several employers; here, we are suggesting systematic, scientifically valid employer surveys. Such surveys would enable policymakers to determine, for instance, whether employers have reservations about hiring Qatari workers and what steps would be required to allay any such concerns.

1998 Cohort Interview Protocol

On the following pages, we reproduce the English version of the survey administered in Arabic to a sample of Qataris who left secondary school in 1998.

NOTE TO INTERVIEWERS: YOU CAN PARAPHRASE THE INTRODUCTORY REMARKS, BUT BE
SURE TO MENTION THE POINTS IN BOLD below. PLEASE GIVE THE ONE-PAGE PROJECT
SUMMARY TO THE RESPONDENT BEFORE OR AFTER THE INTERVIEW.

One of the Qatari government's main concerns is the provision of a high-
quality, modern education for its citizens. Qatar's future depends on
citizens whose training and education prepares them to contribute effectively
to Qatari society throughout their lives, both socially and economically.
Qatar has recently undertaken a number of steps toward improving educational
opportunities, for example with the establishment of the Education City and
the reforms of Qatar University and the K-12 school system. However, the
available offerings may still be insufficient to prepare Qataris to meet the
nation's social and economic needs. The Supreme Education Council has asked
RAND to study the current situation, in order to help them develop priorities
for providing the educational offerings Qatar requires.

To carry out this task, we are talking to individuals in the government, in
the school and university systems, and in public and private organizations to
get their views on a number of issues.

We are talking to Qataris about such things as their education and work
experiences, their work aspirations, and how easy or difficult it was to
transition from school or university to work.

I have a number of specific questions to ask you. *Feel free to tell me you
don't know or don't wish to answer a question or to end the interview at any
time.*

**This interview is confidential. However, RAND is also conducting other
studies for Qatar, and the information we gather from you may be shared with
other RAND projects. However, your name will not be attached to this
information, so you will remain anonymous.** *The principle of confidentiality
holds for all RAND projects, and we will not release information that
identifies you personally to anyone outside of RAND.*

Do you have any questions before we begin?

     Interviewer:

     Date:

     Gender of the respondent:

     Time started:

     Time ended:

     Note any problems here:

A. I would like to start the interview by asking you some questions about your social status?

       Single

       Married

       Divorced

       Widow

B. YEAR OF MARRIAGE _____

C. Do you have any children?

       Yes

       No

D. How many children? _____

Now we have some questions about your work experiences:

1. Are you currently employed?

    [Definition of "employment": Work done for pay, including self-employment—does NOT include playing the stock market]

    Yes

    No

2. How many jobs have you had since you finished secondary school? (PROBE: If you don't remember the exact number, did you have one, more than one?), *(check one)*

[Definition of "job": Any work done for pay, including self-employment]

None	**SKIP TO QUESTION 22**
One	**SKIP TO QUESTION 7**
Other (WRITE IN NUMBER)_____	**GO TO THE NEXT QUESTION**
More than 1, but don't know number.	**GO TO THE NEXT QUESTION**
No Response/does not wish to answer	**SKIP TO QUESTION 22**

I would first like to ask you about your <u>first</u> job after finishing secondary school. [If don't recall exact month, get approximate]

3. What month and year did you start your <u>first</u> job?

Month_____ Year_____

4. What month and year did your <u>first</u> job end?

Month_____ Year_____

5. What type of organization did you work for at your <u>first</u> job? (Check one)

NOTE: Interviewer may need to ask follow up question to get specific type—for example if private company, then ask which of the 3 types on list]

☐ For the government (e.g. Ministry of Education)
☐ For a company or organization the government owns or partially owns (e.g., Qatar Petroleum)
☐ For a privately owned charitable or religious organization
☐ For a privately owned company owned by my family
☐ For a privately owned company **not** owned by my family
☐ Other _____ (please describe)

6. What was the title of your <u>first</u> job?

    [WRITE IN HERE]

    [NOTE: IF RESPONDENT IS NOT CURRENTLY EMPLOYED, BUT HAD A JOB, REFER TO 'MOST RECENT' JOB IN THE NEXT QUESTIONS.]
    NOW I HAVE SOME QUESTIONS ABOUT YOUR [MOST RECENT/CURRENT] JOB.

7. When did you start your <u>[most recent/current]</u> job?

    Month_____ Year_____

    [NOTE: IF CURRENTLY EMPLOYED, SKIP TO QUESTION 9]

8. When did your <u>most recent</u> job end?

    Month_____ Year_____

9. What type of organization [did/do] you work for at your [most recent/current] job? (Check one)

    [NOTE: Interviewer may need to ask follow up question to get specific type—for example if private company, then ask which of 3 types on list]

    ☐ For the government (e.g. Ministry of Education)
    ☐ For a company or organization the government owns or partially owns (e.g., Qatar Petroleum)
    ☐ For a privately owned charitable or religious organization
    ☐ For a privately owned company owned by my family
    ☐ For a privately owned company **not** owned by my family
    ☐ Other _____ (please describe)

10. **What [was/is] the title of your [most recent/current] job?**

(WRITE IN HERE)

11. **What is the LOWEST level of education required to get this job?**
(check one)

☐ Less than Secondary School

☐ Secondary School Degree

☐ Post-secondary diploma (less than BA)

☐ University Degree

☐ Higher diploma (post university, e.g. teaching certificate)
☐ Other _____

☐ No Response

12. **How did you find out about this job?** (check all that apply)

☐ Civil service job placement

☐ Non-governmental job placement service

☐ The school I attended

☐ My family

☐ Friends

☐ Business associate

☐ Newspapers or television

☐ Other sources _____ (please describe)

13. I am interested in which skills and attitudes you think are MOST
IMPORTANT to do your [most recent/current] job. [NOTE: Interviewer
read list and mark yes or no. If face-to-face, give respondent the
handout so they can read along.]

To do this job, do you need?

- Basic math skills (Arithmetic, use calculator)   YES   NO

- Reading and writing (Complete forms, compose memos)   YES   NO

- Advanced math (Algebra, Geometry, Calculus)   YES   NO

- Basic computer skills (word processing, spreadsheets) YES   NO

- Advanced computer skills (computer programming)   YES   NO

- Skills to operate some specific technology/equipment YES   NO

- (SPECIFY TYPE) _____

- to work in a team   YES   NO

- to communicate with outside customers or clients   YES   NO

- to speak English or another foreign language?   YES   NO

- to solve problems, (can you give me an example?)   YES   NO

- to follow directions from a supervisor   YES   NO

- to give directions to other people   YES   NO

- Any other IMPORTANT skills that I have not mentioned? YES   NO

- (Please specify)_____

14. [Did you receive/Have you received] any formal training to learn the skills needed for this job? *(check one)*

- Yes   **GO TO NEXT QUESTION**
- No   **SKIP TO QUESTION 17**
- No Response **SKIP TO QUESTION 17**

15. Where did you receive this training? (check all that apply)

- A Government Training Institute (e.g., IAD)
- A Private Training Facility
- Employer Provided Training Program
- I just decided to get training on my own.
- Other _____

16. Did any of this training occur outside of Qatar?   YES   NO

17. [Did you receive/Have you received] any training on-the-job to learn the skills needed for this job?

- Yes   **GO TO NEXT QUESTION**
- No   **SKIP TO QUESTION 19**
- No response **SKIP TO QUESTION 19**

18. Are you satisfied with the training you [received/have received thus far] on your [most recent/current] job? Or do you think you [would have benefited/would benefit] from more training?

- Yes, am satisfied (skip to Q20)
- No, would like more training

19. In what skill areas do you think you [might have benefited/might benefit] from more training to do your [most recent/current] job?

    [NOTE; no need to read list, check responses or note 'other']

- Basic math skills (Arithmetic, use calculator) YES   NO
- Reading and writing (Complete forms, compose memos)   YES   NO
- Advanced math (Algebra, Geometry, Calculus)   YES   NO
- Basic computer skills (word processing, spreadsheets) YES   NO
- Advanced computer skills (computer programming)   YES   NO
- Skills to operate some specific technology/equipment YES   NO
- (SPECIFY TYPE) _____

•	to work in a team	YES	NO
•	to communicate with outside customers or clients	YES	NO
•	Speak English	YES	NO
•	Solve problems,	YES	NO
•	Follow directions from a supervisor	YES	NO
•	Give directions to other people I work with	YES	NO
•	Other skills I haven't mentioned	YES	NO
•	(Please Specify) _____		

20. Are there any specific skills that you think you need to acquire in order to advance in your job or get a better future job?

[NOTE; no need to read list, check responses or note 'other']

•	Basic math skills (Arithmetic, use calculator) YES	NO	
•	Reading and writing (Complete forms, compose memos)	YES	NO
•	Advanced math (Algebra, Geometry, Calculus)	YES	NO
•	Basic computer skills (word processing, spreadsheets)	YES	NO
•	Advanced computer skills (computer programming)	YES	NO
•	Skills to operate some specific technology/equipment	YES	NO
•	(SPECIFY TYPE) _____		
•	to work in a team	YES	NO
•	to communicate with outside customers or clients	YES	NO
•	Speak English	YES	NO
•	Solve problems	YES	NO
•	Follow directions from a supervisor	YES	NO
•	Give directions to other people I work with	YES	NO
•	Other skills I haven't mentioned	YES	NO
•	Please specify _____		

21. Now I have some questions about what factors are important to you in your choice of a job or career. I am going to read a list of items, and I would like you to tell me if the item is 'not important' 'somewhat important', 'very important' or 'extremely important' in ░▒▓▒░▒▓░░░░░░░
░░

(circle one number in each row)

Category	Not Important	Somewhat Important	Very Important	Extremely Important	Don't Know
Salary	1	2	3	4	0
Bonuses	1	2	3	4	0
Retirement benefits	1	2	3	4	0
Housing benefits	1	2	3	4	0
Other benefits (transportation, marriage, hardship)	1	2	3	4	0
Vacations	1	2	3	4	0
Friendly colleagues	1	2	3	4	0
Job security	1	2	3	4	0
Mixed-gender work environment	1	2	3	4	0
Single-gender work environment	1	2	3	4	0
Working hours	1	2	3	4	0
Opportunity to get more training	1	2	3	4	0
Opportunities for career advancement	1	2	3	4	0
Prestige	1	2	3	4	0
Make a contribution to Society	1	2	3	4	0
Interesting work	1	2	3	4	0
Challenging Work	1	2	3	4	0
Allows time to be with the family	1	2	3	4	0
Makes me feel respected and appreciated	1	2	3	4	0

22. **Now I have some statements about school and work. Thinking about your experiences since high school graduation, I would like to know if you 'completely disagree', 'disagree somewhat', 'agree somewhat' or 'completely agree' with each statement. If you are not sure, just tell me.**

[**NOTE**: if face-to-face give handout to respondent to look at as you read down the list]

(circle one number in each row)

Category	Completely disagree	Disagree somewhat	Agree somewhat	Completely agree	Don't Know
It is important to get a good education	1	2	3	4	0
Getting good grades at school helps you get a better job	1	2	3	4	0
You have to go abroad to get the best education	1	2	3	4	0
People think better of you if you have a university degree	1	2	3	4	0
There should be more jobs open to women	1	2	3	4	0
The best jobs in Qatar are in the government	1	2	3	4	0
People who study a technical field (e.g., engineering) can get a higher paying job.	1	2	3	4	0
Work is harder in private companies than in government jobs	1	2	3	4	0
To get a good job, who you know is more important than what you know	1	2	3	4	0

NOW I HAVE A FEW QUESTIONS ABOUT YOUR EDUCATION

23. Thinking back to your secondary school education, what was your
    "major" field of study? *(check one)*

    ☐ Science

    ☐ Literature, Mathematics, and Science

    ☐ French Literature

    ☐ Industrial

    ☐ Commercial

    ☐ Religious Studies

    ☐ No Response

24. What is your current level of education? *(check one)*

    ☐ Secondary school graduate

    ☐ post secondary school Diploma

    ☐ University/ BA degree

    ☐ Higher Diploma (e.g., teaching certificate)

    ☐ Master's degree

    ☐ A Ph.D. or equivalent

    ☐ Other _____

    ☐ No Response

25. Are you currently enrolled in school? *(check one)*

    ☐ Yes   **SKIP TO QUESTION 28**

    ☐ No   **GO TO NEXT QUESTION**

    ☐ No Response   **GO TO NEXT QUESTION**

26. As things stand now, do you think you will go further in your
    schooling? *(check one)*

    ☐ Yes   **GO TO THE NEXT QUESTION**

□ I Don't know/maybe   **SKIP TO QUESTION 28**

□ No   **SKIP TO QUATION 28**

□ No Response   **GO TO THE NEXT QUESTION**

NOTES:

IF RESPONDENT IS CURRENTLY EMPLOYED BUT DID NOT ATTEND ANY SCHOOL AFTER SECONDARY, END THE INTERVIEW HERE.

IF RESPONDENT IS NOT CURRENTLY EMPLOYED, AND DID NOT ATTEND ANY SCHOOL AFTER SECONDARY, CONTINUE WITH 'CURRENTLY NOT EMPLOYED SUPPLEMENT'

WHETHER RESPOMDENT IS CURRENYLY EMPLOYED OR UNEMPLOYED, BUT ATTENDED ANY SCHOOL AFTER SECONDARY, PLEASE CONTINUE THE INTERVIEW

27. **What do you expect will be the highest educational level you will complete, after you have finished all your schooling (including any future education)**

    □ Secondary

    □ Diploma

    □ University

    □ Higher Diploma

    □ Master's degree

    □ A Ph.D. or equivalent

    □ Other (write in)_____

    □ No Response

28. **What are/are there any your reasons for not pursuing additional education?**

• Unaware of any offerings	yes	no
• Available offerings not useful/interesting	yes	no
• Too inconvenient	yes	no
• Family responsibilities	yes	no
• Health problems	yes	no

- Not interested/did not do well in school   yes   no
- I was not eligible for a scholarship   yes   no
- I can't afford to pay for it   yes   no
- Other _____

29. **I am interested in the <u>first</u> HIGHER EDUCATION INSTUTION you attended after leaving secondary school. If you are currently enrolled in <u>this</u> institution, please provide information on this institution.**

- What is the name of the School? (write in):

- Where is it located? (write in city and country):

- When did you enter this school? (month and year)

30. **What kind of school is this?** *(check one)* **[Note: Interviewer may need to ask further questions to determine if institution offers BA or not]**

☐ Vocational, trade, business, or other career training school

☐ four-year institution leading to a B.A. or B.S. degree

☐ Other (write in) _____

31. **Did you receive any kind of scholarship, fellowship, or grant (not a loan) to go to this school?**

- Yes   **Go to the next question**
- No   **Go to the question 33**

32. **What kind of scholarship was it?**

(WRITE IN)_____

33. **What was your field of study (major)?**

   * Business administration
   * Art and Design
   * Medicine, nursing, or other medical field (e.g. radiology)
   * Law
   * Education
   * Mathematics/Science
   * Sharia/Islamic Studies
   * Engineering
   * Social Science
   * Humanities, Arts, Literature
   * Other (write in)_____

* No Response

34. **What kind of degree or certificate were you studying for?** *(check one)*

   ☐ None
   ☐ Diploma
   ☐ University
   ☐ Higher Diploma
   ☐ Master's degree
   ☐ A Ph.D. or equivalent
   ☐ Other (write in)_____
   ☐ No Response

35. **Did you receive that certificate or degree?** *(check one)*

   * Yes
   * No

36. **Have you attended any other higher education institutions since leaving secondary school?** *(check one)*

   * Yes   **GO TO THE NEXT QUESTION**

- No   [IF RESPONDENT IS NOT CURRENTLY EMPLOYED (QUESTION 1) THE
  GO TO 'CURRENTLY NOT EMPLOYED SUPPLEMENT']

OTHERWISE, END THE INTERVIEW HERE

37. Please provide the following information about the *MOST RECENT*
    higher education institution you attended after leaving secondary
    school. If you are <u>currently</u> enrolled in school, please provide
    information on this school.

- School name (write in):

- Location (write in city and country):

- Month and year entered (write in):

38. During the last month you attended this school, what kind of degree
    or certificate were you studying for? *(check one)*

☐ None
☐ Secondary
☐ Diploma
☐ University
☐ Higher Diploma
☐ Master's degree
☐ A Ph.D. or equivalent
☐ Other (write in)
☐ No Response

39. Did you receive that certificate or degree? *(check one)*

- Yes
- No

```
    --------------------------------------------------------------
----
```

[NOTE:IF NOT CURRENTLY EMPLOYED (RESPONSE TO Q1="NO") ADMINISTER THE QUESTIONS ON THE CURRENTLY NOT EMPLOYED SUPPLEMENT]

```
    --------------------------------------------------------------
----
```

OTHERWISE, END THE INTERVIEW AND THANK INTERVIEWEE FOR HIS OR HER TIME

CURRENTLY NOT EMPLOYED SUPPLEMENT

[NOTE: FOR RESPONDENTS WHO ARE NOT CURRENTLY EMPLOYED (RESPOND "NO" TO QUESTION 1 ON THE MAIN INTERVIEW), ASK THE FOLLOWING QUESTIONS AFTER THE MAIN INTERVIEW]

S1.   Are you currently looking for employment? *(check one)*

- Yes   GO TO NEXT QUESTION
- No   SKIP TO QUESTION S4

S2.   At what types of employers are you looking for work (mark all that apply)?

☐ Government (e.g. Ministry of Education)

☐ Company or organization the government owns or partially owns (e.g., Qatar Petroleum)

☐ Privately-owned charitable or religious organization

☐ Privately-owned company owned by my family

☐ Privately-owned company **not** owned by my family

☐ Other _____ (please describe)

S3.   There are many different reasons why it may be difficult for a person to find the type of job they want. Can you tell me if you feel the following reasons apply to you?

[NOTE: INTERVIEWER, READ LIST OR IF FACE-TO-FACE, GIVE HANDOUT]

(circle one number in each row)

	yes	no	don't know
a. Not enough job openings	1	2	0
b. Available jobs pay too little	1	2	0
c. Do not have skills for available jobs	1	2	0
d. Too many hours to work required at available jobs	1	2	0
e. Social position of available jobs unacceptable	1	2	0
f. high competition for jobs I am looking for	1	2	0
g. Lack of family and/or personal connections	1	2	0
h. Child care not available	1	2	0

[NOTE: IF RESPONDENT IS LOOKING FOR EMPLOYMENT, SKIP TO QUESTION S6]
IF NOT LOOKING FOR WORK (FROM QUESTION) ASK NEXT QUESTION

S4.   I am interested in what factors matter in your decision not to work. Can you tell me if the following factors matter or not?

	yes	no	don't know
a. Family responsibilities	1	2	0
b. Health problems prevent work			
c. Societal/parental Expectations			
d. Don't enjoy work			
e. Other activities (such as investing in stocks) more lucrative			
f. don't have the education or training I need			
g. Other reasons? (write in)			

S5.   If you had better training and education, would you be more interested in working? *(check one)*

Yes   GO TO NEXT QUESTION
No   END INTERVIEW HERE
No Response END INTERVIEW HERE

S6.   Do you plan on pursuing additional education or training to acquire the skill you think you need? *(check one)*

Yes   GO TO NEXT QUESTION

SKIP TO QUESTION S8

No Response **END INTERVIEW HERE**

S7.   What kind of training or education do you intend to pursue?
(check all that apply)

☐ Formal schooling (e.g., at QU)

☐ Job training (e.g. at a MoCSAH training center)

☐ Foreign language skills (English, other?)

☐ Computer training

☐ Other (WRITE IN HERE) _____

S8.   What are your reasons for not pursing additional education
or training? *(check all that apply)*

Unaware of any offerings	yes	no
Available offerings not useful for the skills I need	yes	no
Too inconvenient	yes	no
Family responsibilities	yes	no
Health problems	yes	no
Not interested in/did not do well in school	yes	no
I was not eligible for a scholarship	yes	no
I can't afford to pay for it	yes	no
other _____	yes	no

END OF INTERVIEW: THANK RESPONDENT FOR HIS OR HER TIME

Bibliography

Bound, John, Charles Brown, and Nancy Mathiowetz (2001). "Measurement Error in Survey Data." In James Heckman and Edward Leamer, eds., *Handbook of Econometrics,* Vol. 5, New York: Elsevier Science.

Brewer, Dominic J., Catherine H. Augustine, Gail L. Zellman, Gery Ryan, Charles A. Goldman, Cathleen Stasz, and Louay Constant (2007). *Education for a New Era: Design and Implementation of K–12 Education Reform in Qatar.* Santa Monica, Calif.: RAND Corporation, MG-548-QATAR. As of April 30, 2007: http://www.rand.org/pubs/monographs/MG548/

Bureau of Labor Statistics (2006). "Number of Jobs Held, Labor Market Activity, and Earnings Growth Among the Youngest Baby Boomers: Results from a Longitudinal Survey Summary." USDL 06-1496. As of June 13, 2007: http://www.bls.gov/news.release/nlsoy.nr0.htm

——— (2007). "Employment Status of the Civilian Noninstitutional Population by Age, Sex, and Race. 2006." As of June 13, 2007: ftp://ftp.bls.gov/pub/special.requests/lf/aat3.txt

CIA (2005). *Qatar Country Profile.* As of June 25, 2007: https://www.cia.gov/library/publications/the-world-factbook/geos/qa.html

Gingrich, Andre (1995). "The Prophet's Smile and Other Puzzles: Studying Arab Tribes and Comparing Close Marriages." *Social Anthropology,* Vol. 3, No. 2, pp. 147–170.

International Labour Organization (2004). "International Standard Classification of Occupations: Summary of Major Groups." As of March 25, 2008: http://www.ilo.org/public/english/bureau/stat/isco/isco88/

Kessler, Ronald C., Roderick J. A. Little, and Robert M. Groves (1995). "Advances in Strategies for Minimizing and Adjusting for Survey Nonresponse." *Epidemiologic Reviews,* Vol. 17, No. 1, pp. 192–204.

Nafi, Zuhair Ahmed (1983). *Economic and Social Development in Qatar,* London: Continuum International Publishing.

Planning Council, State of Qatar (2002). *Sample Labour Force Survey, April 2001,* Doha, Qatar: State of Qatar Planning Council.

——— (2005). *A Labour Market Strategy for the State of Qatar: Main Report,* Vol. 1, December 2005.

Rathmell, Andrew, and Kirsten Schulze (2000). "Political Reform in the Gulf: The Case of Qatar." *Middle Eastern Studies,* Vol. 36, No. 4, pp. 47–62.

Romero, Simon (2005). "Natural Gas Powering Qatar Economic Boom: Growth Likened to the Saudi Oil Bonanza." *International Herald Tribune,* Thursday, December 22, 2005.

Stasz, Cathleen, Eric Eide, and Francisco Martorell (2007). *Post-Secondary Education in Qatar: Employer Demand, Student Choice, and Options for Policy.* Santa Monica, Calif.: RAND Corporation, MG-644-QATAR. As of March 20, 2008: http://www.rand.org/pubs/monographs/MG644/

Statistisches Bundesamt Deutschland (2007). "ILO Labour Market Statistics: Unemployment Rates." As of June 15, 2007:
http://www.destatis.de/jetspeed/portal/cms/Sites/destatis/Internet/EN/Content/Statistics/TimeSeries/EconomicIndicators/LabourMarket/Content100/arb440a,templateId=renderPrint.psml

Winckler, Onn (2000). *Population Growth, Migration, and Socio-Demographic Policies in Qatar: Data and Analysis*. Tel Aviv, Israel: Moshe Dayan Center for Middle Eastern and African Studies, Tel Aviv University.